anythink

DESERT
ECOSYSTEMS

by Mirella S. Miller

12-Story Library is an imprint of Bookstaves and Press Room Editions

Produced for 12-Story Library by Red Line Editorial

Photographs ©: Jon Manjeot/Shutterstock Images, cover, 1; Ilyshev Dmitry/Shutterstock Images, 4; Perfect Lazybones/Shutterstock Images, 5; Anton Foltin/Shutterstock Images, 6; Alexxxey/Shutterstock Images, 7; apdesign/Shutterstock Images, 8; Erik Harrison/Shutterstock Images, 9; Volodymyr Goinyk/Shutterstock Images, 10; Galyna Andrushko/Shutterstock Images, 11; Kris Wiktor/Shutterstock Images, 12; EcoPrint/Shutterstock Images, 13; Kelly vanDellen/Shutterstock Images, 14; IrinaK/Shutterstock Images, 15; Chris Watson/Shutterstock Images, 16; creativex/Shutterstock Images, 17; Kathryn Roach/Shutterstock Images, 18; Oleg Znamenskiy/Shutterstock Images, 19; sumikophoto/Shutterstock Images, 20, 29 (top left); Lorcel/Shutterstock Images, 21, 28 (middle); Cat Downie/Shutterstock Images, 22; Matej Kastelic/Shutterstock Images, 23; phoelixDE/Shutterstock Images, 24; bikeriderlondon/Shutterstock Images, 25; Zack Frank/Shutterstock Images, 26; Cinematographer/Shutterstock Images, 27; NPS/Michael Vamstad, 28 (top); NPS/Michael Quinn, 28 (bottom); Peter Paquet/Northwest Power and Conservation Council CC2.0, 29 (top right); MartinaPal/iStockphoto, 29 (bottom left); NPS/Brad Sutton, 29 (bottom right)

Content Consultant: Nicholas Lancaster, Affiliate Research Professor, Division of Earth and Ecosystem Sciences, Desert Research Institute

Library of Congress Cataloging-in-Publication Data
Names: Miller, Mirella S.
Title: Desert ecosystems / by Mirella S. Miller.
Description: Mankato, MN : 12-Story Library, [2018] | Series: Earth's
    ecosystems | Audience: Grade 4 to 6. | Includes bibliographical references
    and index.
Identifiers: LCCN 2016052220 (print) | LCCN 2016053520 (ebook) | ISBN
    9781632354549 (hardcover : alk. paper) | ISBN 9781632355201 (pbk. : alk.
    paper) | ISBN 9781621435723 (hosted e-book)
Subjects: LCSH: Desert ecology--Juvenile literature. | Desert
    animals--Juvenile literature. | Desert plants--Juvenile literature.
Classification: LCC QH541.5.D4 M55 2018 (print) | LCC QH541.5.D4 (ebook) |
    DDC 577.54--dc23
LC record available at https://lccn.loc.gov/2016052220

Printed in China
022017

Access free, up-to-date content on this topic plus a full digital version of this book. Scan the QR code on page 31 or use your school's login at 12StoryLibrary.com.

Table of Contents

Deserts Cover a Quarter of Earth

Desert ecosystems are found around the world. They are large, dry spaces. Very little rain falls in these areas. Most deserts are located close to the equator. They are found in both the northern and southern hemispheres. Deserts cover approximately one-quarter of Earth's land surface. Only specially adapted plants and animals live in these ecosystems.

Scientists have found evidence that deserts may not have been as dry in ancient times. This means more humans could have lived in them. Archaeologists have found paintings, tools, and fossils in deserts around the world. These fossils show how desert life has changed

The Tatacoa Desert is found in Colombia.

Some deserts include large sand dunes.

over time. A wider variety of plants and animals once grew and lived in these ecosystems.

Climate change is one reason desert ecosystems are different today than in the past. It includes changes in average temperatures, winds, or rainfall. Changes in weather patterns warm or cool the planet. Some deserts have periods of more rain than in the past. At other times, deserts are drier. As Earth's climate continues to change, so will desert ecosystems.

20.9 million

Area, in square miles (54.1 million sq km), of land deserts cover on Earth.

- Deserts are large, dry spaces.
- Little rain falls in deserts.
- Deserts cover approximately one-quarter of Earth's land surface.

THINK ABOUT IT

Think about the place where you live. Is it a desert ecosystem? Write down two or three characteristics of the ecosystem of your city or town.

Little Rain Falls in the Desert

Desert ecosystems have minimal moisture and rainfall. High temperatures, wind, and low humidity add to the low moisture levels. Air temperatures are often higher than 100 degrees Fahrenheit (38°C). But the desert ground is even warmer. This is because the sun's heat is absorbed by the dry earth. If there was moisture in the ground, some of the heat would be used in the process of evaporation.

Desert winds can be quite strong. This is because there are few trees and plants to break the wind. Desert winds are typically hot and have no moisture. They blow

The Sonoran Desert covers large parts of the southwestern United States and northwestern Mexico.

Wadi Rum is a desert in Jordan.

dust and sand across the landscape. They block clouds from forming and making rain. This makes deserts even drier.

When rain does fall in the desert, plants and animals thrive. Rain is not the only moisture that may be useful to plants and animals. Fog is common in coastal deserts. Dew found on plants also provides moisture in a desert ecosystem.

DESERT RAINS

Deserts near the equator get most of their rain in the summertime. This includes the southern Sahara Desert in North Africa and the Chihuahuan and Sonoran Deserts in Mexico and the United States. Deserts farther from the equator have more rainfall in the winter.

20

Average maximum number of days that rain falls in a desert each year.

- Desert ecosystems do not get much rainfall.
- Winds in the desert are hot and dry.
- Fog and dew provide moisture in deserts.

Rocks and Sand Cover Desert Areas

Desert environments have many things in common. All of them are dry places. The soil is weak and cannot support much plant life, but some bacteria live in it.

Many deserts are covered by areas of sand. The sand is not tightly compacted. It is loose and moves easily. The wind often blows sand into dunes. These dunes move constantly. Sand-covered deserts

Winds help shape sandy desert landscapes into dunes.

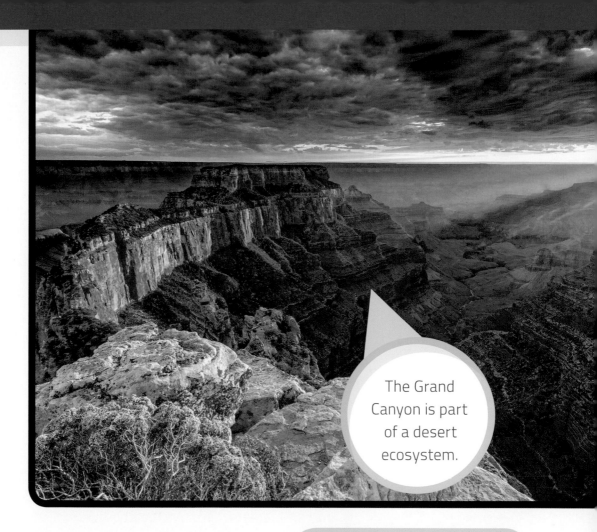

The Grand Canyon is part of a desert ecosystem.

are the most challenging desert landscapes. It is hard for plants and animals to survive in them.

Not all deserts are sandy. These ecosystems actually have a variety of landscapes. Some deserts are made up of stony plains. Gravel and stones cover the landscape. These rocks have a shiny dark finish. Other deserts have rocky mountains. No soil is found in mountainous desert environments.

10
Percentage of Earth's deserts that are made up of sand dunes.

- All desert environments are dry.
- Sand, gravel, and stones cover parts of many deserts.
- Many deserts have stony plains and steep mountain ranges.

4

Deserts Are Found All around the World

Desert ecosystems are not limited to one part of the world. They are found on all continents, except Europe. Even Antarctica is a desert. It is considered the driest continent. There is little rain or snow there. The snow that does fall never melts.

Deserts in Africa are located in the northern and southern parts of the continent. The Sahara in the north covers about 25 percent of Africa's land. The Kalahari and Namib are other large deserts in southern Africa.

Asia has many deserts. They cover parts of Iran, China, Mongolia, India, and Pakistan. The Arabian and Gobi Deserts are the two largest deserts in Asia. Both are extremely hot in summer. Australia has four deserts. The Great Victoria Desert is the largest. It is in western and southern Australia.

Antarctica is the driest place on Earth.

The Gobi Desert spreads across northern China and southern Mongolia.

The Americas are also home to many desert ecosystems. Deserts found in North America are mainly located in the West. The Great Basin Desert covers 190,000 square miles (492,000 sq km) of the southwestern United States. It is the largest desert in the United States. Much of Arizona and parts of Mexico are home to the Sonoran Desert.

In South America, the two largest deserts are the Patagonian and the Atacama. The Patagonian Desert is found mostly in southern Argentina. Chile and Peru are home to the Atacama Desert. This desert is known for its beautiful landscapes.

3.3 million

Area, in square miles (8.5 sq km), of land the Sahara Desert covers.

- Antarctica is the driest of all the continents.
- Deserts in Africa are located in the north and the south.
- There are many deserts in Asia.

Animals Burrow in Cool Places

Deserts have harsh environments. But some animals are able to survive in these ecosystems. Rodents are some of the most common animals in desert areas. These small mammals can easily burrow underground. The ground's surface may be hot, but underneath the ground it is cooler. Rodents may come above ground at night. They take advantage of the cooler temperatures to hunt for food.

The Gila monster is a venomous lizard that lives in the Sonoran Desert.

Reptiles are another common animal in desert ecosystems. Most deserts have a variety of lizards and snakes, such as Gila monsters, bearded dragons, and rattlesnakes. Like rodents, reptiles are burrowing animals. They bury themselves underground in extreme heat.

Although it is easier for small animals to avoid the sun, larger animals also call the desert home. Mammals such as gazelles, foxes, hyenas, coyotes, mule deer, and wild pigs are some of the animals that can survive in desert conditions.

During very dry periods, some larger desert mammals move to nearby mountains. There, they can stay cooler and find water more easily. Australia's deserts are home to certain marsupial species, such as kangaroos and wallabies.

140

Approximate number of marsupial species in Australia.

- Rodents burrow underground to stay cool.
- Gazelles, foxes, hyenas, coyotes, mule deer, and wild pigs are some of the larger animals that live in the desert.
- During extremely dry periods, some animals move to nearby mountains.

The brown hyena lives in the Kalahari Desert in Africa.

Insects and Invertebrates Call the Desert Home

A wide variety of insects live in desert ecosystems. The Great Basin Desert is the largest in the United States. It is also home to a national park. Scientists at Great Basin National Park in Nevada have studied and tracked the park's insects for years. There are more than 100 butterfly species. There are also beetles, ants, and flies.

Cockroaches are one insect commonly found in many desert ecosystems. Some cockroaches do not need much water to survive. They eat dead plants for nutrients. Many cockroaches live under rocks. They prefer dark environments.

Black swallowtail butterflies are found in Great Basin National Park.

50
Number of beetle species in the Great Basin Desert.

- Scientists at Great Basin National Park have studied and tracked insects for years.
- More than 100 butterfly species have been identified in the park.
- Some types of cockroaches need little water to drink.
- Jumping spiders live in the Sonoran Desert.

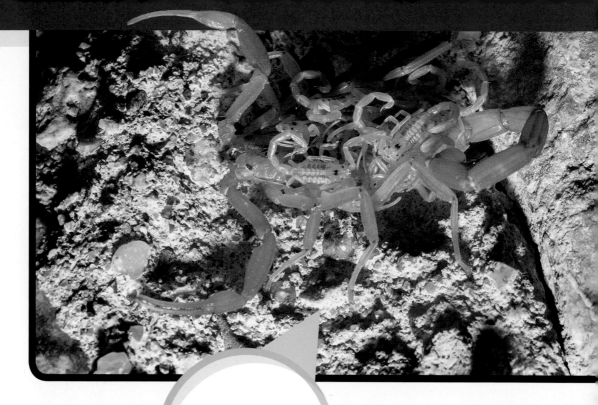

Arizona bark scorpions live in the Sonoran Desert.

Spiders and scorpions are two larger types of invertebrates found in deserts. Wolf spiders and black widow spiders have been seen in Great Basin National Park. Jumping spiders live in the Sonoran Desert. They jump to catch or chase their prey. These species need little water to survive.

Other invertebrates that call the desert home include centipedes and millipedes. Centipedes are nocturnal. They eat worms, snails, and crickets. Millipedes eat dying plants. They look for cool, damp places to live. In the desert, they take shelter under rocks.

BURROWING BEETLES

The cactus longhorn beetle makes its home in saguaro cacti in the Sonoran Desert. Beneath the surface of the cacti, the beetles create tunnels. They eat saguaro seedlings before the cacti can start to grow.

Birds Soar through the Sky

Birds do well in desert environments. They can easily move from place to place in search of food and water. They soar through the skies to keep cool. Finches and pigeons are the most common birds in deserts. Australia also has many desert parrots.

While most desert birds fly, they have other ways of moving to use less energy.

Some birds hop from rock to rock in search of food. Other birds peck holes into giant cacti to beat the heat. They build nests and get relief from the sun inside these cacti. To deal with dry conditions, many birds may migrate to find water.

The cactus wren lives in the Sonoran Desert. It eats seeds, ants, and other insects it finds beneath rocks. It builds its nest using grasses and other plants. These nests are often found inside cacti.

Australian ringneck parrots can be found in the deserts of Australia.

Quails spend most of their time at the bottom of mountains found in the Sonoran Desert. Often there is more water in these areas. Quails change their diets with the seasons. This means they do not need to migrate to find food. They eat whatever they can find. This includes seeds, fruit, and insects. These items are available year-round in the desert.

Elf owls live in deserts. They are able to see well in the dark. This means they hunt well at night. They use their ears to listen for prey. Elf owls do not make noise as they fly. This is a special trait unique to elf owls. They can easily surprise crickets, scorpions, and beetles.

Elf owls live in Mexico and the southwestern United States.

THINK ABOUT IT

How are birds able to survive desert conditions? List a few reasons, and explain why.

5
Height, in inches (13 cm), of an elf owl.

- A variety of bird species live in desert ecosystems.
- Cactus wrens build nests inside cacti.
- Quails eat different foods depending on the season.
- Elf owls are silent when they fly.

17

Plants Become Inactive during the Dry Season

Although deserts are dry, many plants can thrive in these ecosystems. They grow quickly and spread easily. This means a plant species will not easily die off. Because of the harsh environment, many individual desert plants have short life cycles. Some plants survive the heat and low water supply by becoming dormant during very dry times of year.

There are many types of desert plants. Lilies cover the deserts in Africa. Carnations grow in Middle Eastern deserts. These plants gather as much moisture as possible when it rains.

The Apache plume is a type of shrub found in the desert.

15

Maximum width, in feet (4.6 m), that an Engelmann prickly pear cactus grows.

- Most species of cacti grow only in deserts found in the Americas.
- Deserts around the world have daisy and bean plants.
- Lilies grow across Africa's deserts.
- Some plants become inactive during dry seasons.

Grasses grow in the Sahara Desert in Egypt.

ADAPTING TO SURVIVE

Desert plants have adapted to the lack of water. Cacti are some of the most recognizable desert plants. However, most species grow only in the Americas. The saguaro and prickly pear are two common cactus plants. Deserts in other parts of the world do not have cactus plants. Many other desert plants also grow only in one part of the world. Other plants are common to multiple deserts. Different types of daisies and bean plants are found in deserts around the world.

Other plants have underground organs similar to roots. They suck up water when it rains to help the plants grow quickly. Larger wooded plants have deep roots to gather water. The most common plants in the Sahara Desert are different types of grasses.

The Mojave Desert Is Home to Diverse Plants and Animals

The Mojave Desert is one of the most diverse deserts on Earth. Many different plants and animals live there. The Mojave Desert is found between the Great Basin and Sonoran Deserts. This is in the western United States.

More than 2,300 different plant species live in the Mojave Desert. The ghost flower is one unique plant found there. It is a see-through flower that does not have nectar. Bees still try to feed from the plant. They carry its pollen to the next flower, helping the plant reproduce.

The greater roadrunner is found in the Mojave Desert.

ANCIENT LIFE IN THE MOJAVE DESERT

American Indians lived in the Mojave Desert for thousands of years. They ate prickly pear cactus and hunted deer and bighorn sheep. They lived along the Colorado River. This was near a major trading route. The American Indians traded their goods with European traders and settlers. Today very few people live in the Mojave Desert.

Joshua Tree National Park is located in southern California.

The desert tortoise and the bighorn sheep are two animals that live in the Mojave. Desert tortoises can live for more than a year without water. Bighorn sheep can go for weeks without it.

The Mojave Desert is covered in low bushes. The desert is part of Joshua Tree National Park. The Joshua tree is a unique plant found only in the Mojave Desert. All Joshua trees look a little different. Some are spiky and without branches. Others are bushy and have branches. The trees have tough leaves. Early American Indians used the leaves to create baskets.

They also ate the flower buds and seeds from Joshua trees.

31,250
Area, in square miles (80,937 sq km), the Mojave Desert covers.

- More than 2,300 different plant species grow in the Mojave Desert.
- The desert is found between the Great Basin and the Sonoran Deserts.
- The Joshua tree can be found only in the Mojave Desert.

21

The Sahara Covers Much of Northern Africa

Outside of Antarctica, the Sahara Desert is the largest desert on Earth. It covers most of northern Africa, including most of Algeria, Egypt, Libya, Mauritania, Niger, and Western Sahara. Mountains, sand dunes, and basins dot the desert landscape. Unlike other deserts, the Sahara has two permanent rivers and a few lakes. The Nile River crosses the Sahara from south to north. The Niger River flows through the southern part of the desert.

The Sahara has high temperatures in the summer months. It can become warmer than 122 degrees Fahrenheit

The fennec fox lives in the Sahara Desert of northern Africa.

Ait Benhaddou is a village in the Sahara Desert.

(50˚C). But during the winter, temperatures drop. Nighttime temperatures can be below freezing from December through February. Approximately three inches (7.6 cm) of rain fall throughout the year. Most rain falls in the winter in the northern Sahara.

The conditions in the Sahara are more extreme than in other deserts around the world. Still, more than 1,000 different plant species grow in the Sahara Desert. Grasses and bushes are the most common plants. Olive trees grow in some areas of the desert. The Sahara is also home to many animals. Cobra snakes and crocodiles live in desert basins. Gazelles and deer run across the dunes. More than 300 types of birds fly through the skies.

2 million
Estimated number of people who call the Sahara Desert home.

- Other than Antarctica, the Sahara is the largest desert on Earth.
- More than 1,000 plant species grow in the Sahara Desert.
- The northern Sahara gets most of its rain in the winter.

Desertification Affects Desert Ecosystems

Some deserts are growing due to a problem called desertification. The land in other ecosystems is ruined from climate change and human activity. People remove trees and plants from these ecosystems, turning them into deserts. They might be removed to make way for businesses or homes. This process is called desertification.

Desertification can also happen if the land is farmed or grazed too much. It is stressful for plants, animals, and the soil. They cannot thrive in places that have been harmed by human activity.

Desertification is happening near the Sahara, in parts of Australia, and in parts of Asia and North America. Losing the plants, animals,

Climate change and human activity affect desert ecosystems.

and water resources is harmful for people living in these places.

People sometimes hurt desert ecosystems. They may remove plants and bushes. They may collect wood for fires or heating their homes. They may own animals whose hooves ruin the soil. Litter is another negative factor affecting deserts.

People sometimes dump trash in deserts.

NEGATIVE IMPACTS

Human activity has one of the largest negative impacts on deserts. Military forces are sometimes stationed near deserts. They use large, off-road vehicles with big tires that can be harmful to the desert. The sand and desert soil are fragile. People sometimes mine desert areas. The digging can be very stressful on desert soil. Off-road vehicles, such as dirt bikes and four-wheel-drive trucks, also damage the desert.

10 to 20
Percentage of deserts that are affected by desertification.

- Desertification happens when other ecosystems are damaged and become deserts.
- The Sahara, most of Australia's deserts, and parts of Asia and North America are affected by desertification.
- The loss of resources is harmful to people living in these ecosystems.

25

People Can Help Save the World's Deserts

People can help save deserts from becoming damaged or destroyed. The World Wildlife Federation (WWF) is working to save deserts. The WWF is an international group. It raises money to help conservation efforts. The WWF's first step in working to save deserts is solving the water issue in these ecosystems. Water sources need to be preserved. Human activity is ruining them. They have not been properly taken care of.

One of the places the WWF is working on water flow is in the Chihuahuan Desert. This desert is in the southwestern United States and Mexico. The Rio Grande River flows through the desert. Many people rely on it for drinking and to water crops. But it is being threatened by evaporation and invasive species. People have built dozens of dams along the river, too. The WWF has set up protected areas to help the river thrive.

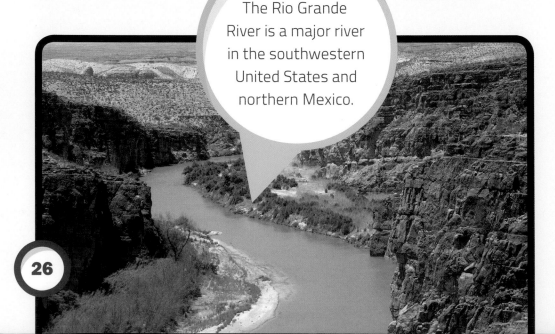

The Rio Grande River is a major river in the southwestern United States and northern Mexico.

The Nazca Desert is in southern Peru.

In Peru, human activity is threatening the deserts. The population is growing, and the country is popular with tourists. The WWF is working with the government to patrol desert areas and do wildlife surveys.

Local volunteers living in and around the Sonoran Desert work to protect their ecosystem from potential threats. They monitor wildlife cameras, clean up litter, and raise money to preserve the desert. They want to keep the ecosystem as healthy as possible. Working together as a community has helped protect this desert ecosystem.

130
Number of mammal species in the Chihuahuan Desert.

- The World Wildlife Federation is working to save deserts.
- The organization is working on water flow in the Chihuahuan Desert.
- The WWF protects desert areas from harmful human activity.
- Volunteers around the Sonoran Desert work to clean up and protect it.

THINK ABOUT IT

What factors are harming deserts? What actions can people take to help save them? Make a list of three actions.

Desert Food Web

Joshua tree

coyote

bighorn sheep

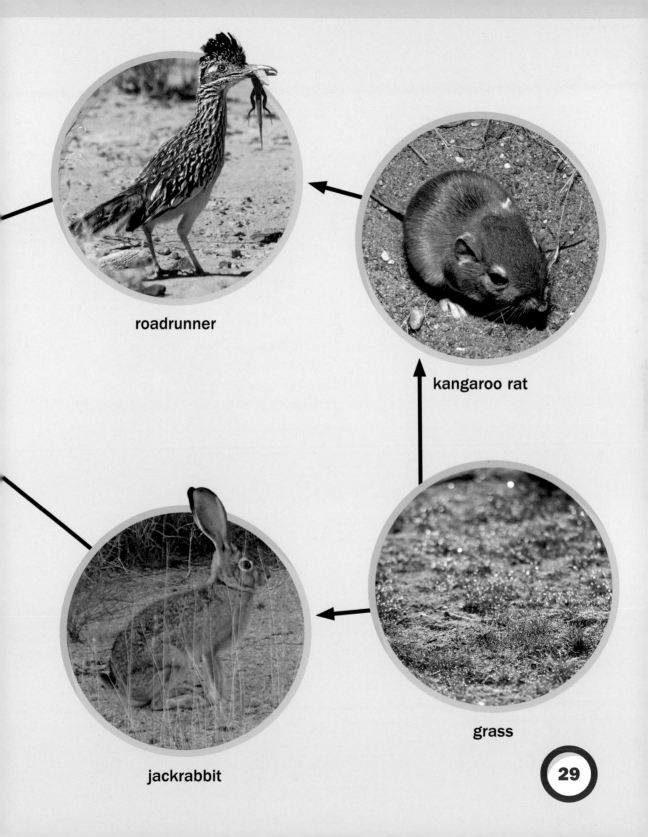

roadrunner

kangaroo rat

grass

jackrabbit

29

Glossary

adapted
Changed to fit a situation.

burrow
A hole in the ground that is made by an animal.

gravel
Small pieces of rock.

inactive
Not involving physical energy or movement.

mammals
Types of animals that are covered in fur or hair and feed their young milk.

marsupial
A type of mammal; females have a pouch to carry their young.

migrate
To move from one area to another at different times of the year.

nocturnal
Most active at night.

organs
Parts of an organism that have a certain function.

prey
An animal that is hunted or killed for food.

For More Information

Books

Benoit, Peter. *Deserts*. New York: Children's Press, 2011.

Cohen, Marina. *Deserts Inside Out*. New York: Crabtree Publishing Company, 2015.

Gagne, Tammy. *Desert Ecosystems*. Minneapolis, MN: Abdo Publishing, 2016.

Visit 12StoryLibrary.com

Scan the code or use your school's login at **12StoryLibrary.com** for recent updates about this topic and a full digital version of this book. Enjoy free access to:

- Digital ebook
- Breaking news updates
- Live content feeds
- Videos, interactive maps, and graphics
- Additional web resources

Note to educators: Visit 12StoryLibrary.com/register to sign up for free premium website access. Enjoy live content plus a full digital version of every 12-Story Library book you own for every student at your school.

Index

About the Author

Mirella S. Miller is an author and editor of several children's books. She lives in Minnesota with her husband and their dogs. One of her favorite places to visit is the Sonoran Desert.